GEMATRIA

JEROME ROTHENBERG

GEMATRIA

PS3568
.O86
G46
1994

SUN &
MOON

CLASSICS

45

SUN *&* MOON PRESS

1994

Sun & Moon Press
A Program of The Contemporary Arts Educational Project, Inc.,
a nonprofit corporation
6026 Wilshire Boulevard, Los Angeles, California 90036

This edition first published in paperback in 1994 by Sun & Moon Press
10   9   8   7   6   5   4   3   2   1
FIRST EDITION
©Jerome Rothenberg, 1994
Biographical information ©Sun & Moon Press, 1994
All rights reserved

This book was made possible, in part, through an operational grant
from the Andrew W. Mellon Foundation and through contributions to
The Contemporary Arts Educational Project, Inc.,a nonprofit corporation

Some of these poems first appeared in the following magazines and anthol-
ogies: *Caliban, Notus, Oovrah, Paper Air, Poésie Internationale Anthologie*
(Luxembourg), *Screens & Tasted Parallels, Shirim, Sulfur, Talus, Theater
Review,* and *Tikkun.* In addition individual poems were published as broad-
sides (*Gematria 482, Tens for David Meltzer, Gematria Five*) by Bellevue
Press (Binghamton, New York), as chapbooks by Spot Press and Tetrad
Press (both in London), and as part of Jerome Rothenberg's *Two Poems,*
published by the St Mark's Poetry Project's *Project Papers.*

Cover: Ian Tyson
Typography: Jim Cook
Design: Katie Messborn

LIBRARY OF CONGRESS CATALOGING IN PUBLICATION DATA
Rothenberg, Jerome (1931)
Gematria
p. cm. — (Sun & Moon Classics: 40)
ISBN 1-55713-097-3
1. Hebrew language—Alphabet—Poetry. 2. Cabala—Poetry. I. Title.
PS3568.086G46   1994
811'.54—dc20   93-29696
CIP

Printed in the United States of America on acid-free paper.

CONTENTS

BEYOND GEMATRIA

POST / FACE

For Edmond Jabès, in memory

The desert
speaks.

Gematria

A GEMATRIA FOR JACKSON MAC LOW

CHANCE

made it happen.

Chance = 310.

3 GEMATRIAS FOR JOHN CAGE

ROARATORIO (1)   ROARATORIO (2)

A new   The leeks
place.   & the fire.

          ROARATORIO (3)

          The magicians
          return.

Roaratorio = 625.

A LANGUAGE GEMATRIA FOR CHARLES BERNSTEIN

Divination.

Like the bed
in the firmament.

Language.

Our voice
& your eye.

Colors
limped.

The thick darkness
shall rule you.

Language
shall rule you.

3 GEMATRIAS FOR ARMAND SCHWERNER

THE TABLETS (1)

Fearing
to give light.

THE TABLETS (2)

The moon
will choose.

THE TABLETS (3)

Sheol
in Sodom.

The Tablets = 443.

2 GEMATRIAS FOR HOWARD NORMAN

WILDERNESS (1)   WILDERNESS (2)

They emptied it out.   Your eyes
                         in the tree.

Wilderness = 400.

TENS, FOR DAVID MELTZER

Ten riches.

Ten fountains.

Ten wrestlings.

Ten cities.

Ten wonders.

Ten hairs.

Ten
& ten.

GEMATRIAS
12 x 22

FIRST GEMATRIA

ENOUGH

or too much.

_____

THE BAT

His yellow
angel.

_____

THE BORDER (1)   THE BORDER (2)

A hundred.   Alone.

_____

EYES

A hole
& an amethyst.

_____

EVENING

Evil.

A FLAG

Living, raw
garments of.

IN THE GARDEN

In the sea.

OUR DREAMS

sprouting
forth.

GOD (1)

A flame.

GOD (2)

A terror.

A HOOK

One part
linen.

THE MAIDEN (1)

Stretched out
& ready.

THE MAIDEN (2)

Compasses
night.

TO THE MOON (1)

The shore
a small matter.

TO THE MOON (2)

Witnesses
below.

THE NEEDY

shall judge.

_____

IN THE SADDLE

Red, ruddy
nuts.

_____

SALT (1)   SALT (2)

A flood.   Like the stars.

SALT (3)

Dreaming.

_____

GEMATRIA 428

I have sinned
into freedom.

_____

IN SODOM (1)

A garden.
A wall.

IN SODOM (2)

At what time
shall we come?

THESE

Those.

IN THE [AMERICAN] TREE

for Ron Silliman

(1)
Dark.
Damsel.
Dan.

(2)
The glorious
anger.

WAILING

A brick
in my mouth.

WITH US

Against us.

SECOND GEMATRIA
"Together"

TOGETHER

A feast
when he came.

IN THE SHADOW (1)　　　IN THE SHADOW (2)

I am　　　　　　　　　A stolen
your mother.　　　　　womb.

THE IDOLS (1)　　　　THE IDOLS (2)

The garden　　　　　who fed you.
is hot.

MY MOUTH

A hole.

LICE (1)

Like fat
from her issue.

LICE (2)

Hollow
& dark.

FOUR

a power
at night

fierce &
full.

GEMATRIA 252

Horses
in Eden.

IN A VISION (1)

A harlot.

IN A VISION (2)

His glory
perhaps.

AN ANGEL (1)   AN ANGEL (2)

The cup,   By himself.
the little owl.

AN ANGEL (3)

Amen.

AS YOU ARE

Λ child
& a poor man.

DEATH (1)   DEATH (2)

The yellow   The moon
angels   like a stranger.
of God.

DEW

A rebuke.

EASTWARD (1)

The mountains.

EASTWARD (2)

A ladder
& flaming.

YOUR FACE

I will know
in a dream.

GEMATRIA 123

A womb
in a vision.

The thief
& the beast.

IN MY MOUTH

Red
terror.

THEIR LIVES (1)

like a garden.

THEIR LIVES (2)

like a stone.

GEMATRIA 20

The falcon.

The hooks.

His hands
will swoop down.

A WOMB (1)

Bruised
& sore.

A WOMB (2)

God
was slain.

SHE SAID:

Bruised
testicles.

A FACE (1)   A FACE (2)

My mouth   I redeem
knew him.   from the sea.

A FACE (3)

kept murmuring.

A MAN WHO SEES

Knowing
a window.

THIRD GEMATRIA
"Lot in Sodom"

THE ADULTERER

He found her.

_____

I COMMAND YOU:

Eat!

_____

FOR A HARLOT (1)

She gave birth
& he rolled.

FOR A HARLOT (2)

Her blood
a measure.

_____

THE STONE

crushed
her hands.

_____

A FINGER (1)

Through his ear,
into her mouth.

_____

A BREAST

I will come
in her hand.

_____

IN A DREAM (1)

To pronounce it unclean.

IN A DREAM (3)

It shall be circumcised.

_____

THE SINNERS

mingled.

_____

A FINGER (2)

To swell
her belly.

IN A DREAM (2)

Sweet unto me, dear.

SODOM (1)

Lewdness
shall cease.

SODOM (2)

Lewdness,
I pray thee.

SODOM (3)

Lewdness—
what is it?

———————————

HIS FORESKIN

& a knob.

———————————

AS HE WRESTLED

The stone
became hot.

———————————

33

HER BELLY (1)

Her strength
when I come.

HER BELLY (2)

& the wheat
at the entrance.

THE TOUCHER

& the one who touches.

TO ONAN (1)

Two days—
then he hardened.

TO ONAN (2)

In their mouths.

IN THE RAIN

Streaked
dainties.

THEIR PORTION (1)

The dream
will perish.

THEIR PORTION (2)

They shall touch
his tail.

A SPIRIT (1)

Rings.
A dark
stone.

A SPIRIT (2)

Onan
commanded him.

HIS VOICE

Alive
in her womb.

PORNOGRAPHIC POEM (1)

A breast
will be glorified.

PORNOGRAPHIC POEM (2)

Goats
will be slain.

PORNOGRAPHIC POEM (3)

What is it?
What is it?

IN THE MORNING (1)

Full
heavy
testicles.

IN THE MORNING (2)

A bird
in your hand.

THE BEARD
for Michael McClure

To eat from
your belly.

A BLOSSOM

Her beautiful
mouth.

FOURTH GEMATRIA
"In the Shadow"

WITHOUT GOD

Without terror.

_____

GEMATRIA 372

Seven.
Plenty.
A week.

_____

MY HEART (1)   MY HEART (2)

Flaming.   Blood.

_____

THE SIGN

I see
a word / spoken.

_____

IN THE SHADOW (1)   IN THE SHADOW (2)

A womb   I am
he devours.   nothing.

TESTIMONY
  for Charles Reznikoff

The light.
The terror.

BURNING

Your beautiful
mind.

Dead
at the entry.

A FOUNTAIN (1)   A FOUNTAIN (2)

An eye.   Shall I hide?

39

A WINDOW

Wherein
& forward.

COLORS (1)

Yellow
stars.

COLORS (2)

His red
throne.

THE CANDLESTICK / THE FIRE

The yellow
Baal
eats
like a god.

A VISION (1)

Beat it
with power.

A VISION (2)

God
is crushed.

YOU

& a double.

THE CITY

Broken.

.

Void.

FLESH (1)

An ark
& a worm.

FLESH (2)

Before
& bitter.

THE ROCK

fell.

A CURSE

Your father
shall live.

A CLOUD (1)

In wood.

A CLOUD (2)

Forever.

ALL

or enough.

CITIES, CITIES

Silver
& speckled.

A tree
fallen down.

My country
a fire.

.

Divided.

THE VOICE (1)　　　　THE VOICE (2)

will answer.　　　　A voice.

FIFTH GEMATRIA
"Among"

AMONG (1)

Spiritum
descended.

AMONG (2)

Breath
trickled down.

———————————————

YOUR SHOES

& the wind.

———————————————

A DOOR (1)

White.

A DOOR (2)

Open.

———————————————

LOUDLY

A bell.

———————————————

They stripped
& let her be.

They stripped
& she came.

———————————————

ROOMS

Those that were numbered.

———————————————

PASSOVER

passed.

———————————————

NIGHT (1)   NIGHT (2)

The melons.   & they rolled.

———————————————

THE LIGHT

Like God
in Sodom.

———————————————

AN INHERITANCE

Shut—
like the rain.

UNDER HIM

Houses of
lusting.

.

United
delight.

GEMATRIA 316

The man
was aroused.

The rod
heated up.

GOING / NUTS

You eat
your face.

THE SHOVELS

Dyed red.

AGAINST YOU

Your anger.
Your anger.

"AND FRAIL WITH LONGING"

As she spoke
I dug it.

THE EGGS (1)   THE EGGS (2)

We came out.   On a stalk.

_____

YOUR SHOES

went walking.

THE EARLY RAIN

& the wood.

_____

THE LIGHTS

Spies
all over.

_____

WORDS
        for William Carlos Williams

A red wheel
barrow.

Your wives
like wives.

.

Birds
in his house.

SIXTH GEMATRIA
"Gematria"

GEMATRIA (1)

To spy out.

GEMATRIA (2)

I will bless them.

GEMATRIA (3)

Shut.

G

_____

ABEL & GOD (1)

A large
banner.

ABEL & GOD (2)

We have sinned.

E

_____

THE CAMEL

Father,
come.

M

_____

LIFE (1)   LIFE (2)

                                                A

Upward   The sword
& after.   in its place.

_____

WHITE (1)   WHITE (2)

A wild ox   Among you.
will tell them.
                                                T

            WHITE (3)

            When they die.

_____

THE LORD (1)   THE LORD (2)

                                                R

will become.   & be.

_____

51

MANKIND

Exceedingly.   I

_____

MASTERY (1)   MASTERY (2)

Half of   Violence
my arrows.   shall cease.

                                                               A

          MASTERY (3)

          The stones
          blot me out.

_____

JEALOUS

A very small   G
god.

_____

KINDLED (1)   KINDLED (2)

Her blood   Thou lovest
became heated.   Goyim.

        KINDLED (3)

                                              E

          The bed
          is hot.

———————————————

LAUGHTER (1)   LAUGHTER (2)

                                              M

Their blood   The window
into his nostrils.   numbed.

———————————————

MY FATHER

One.   A

———————————————

LIGHT (1)　　　　　LIGHT (2)

A stranger.　　　　I will see.

　　　　LIGHT (3)　　　　　　　　　　T

　　　　is great.

_____

A FLAME (1)　　　　A FLAME (2)

　　　　　　　　　　　　　　　　R

Terror.　　　　　　One
　　　　　　　　　　father
　　　　　　　　　　which is coming.

_____

HIS GOD (1)　　HIS GOD (2)　　HIS GOD (3)

　　　　　　　　　　　　　　　　　　　I

A dog.　　　　　A beast.　　　　What is it?

_____

FOR THE HOLY:

An increase
of wonder.   A

_____

THE SONG (1)   THE SONG (2)

                                                    G

The river   A scream
will change.   growing larger.

_____

TERROR (1)   TERROR (2)

                                                    E

A flame.   The hands of
                      a grasshopper.

TERROR (3)

A sacrifice
when you came in.

_____

TURTLE-DOVES

Lamps.   M

_____

WE HAVE COME THROUGH!
                    for D. H. Lawrence
From Eden.   A
From his bosom.

_____

YOUR FATHER (1)   YOUR FATHER (2)
                                                T
Bore the loss of it.   In pain.

_____

FOR A WITNESS (1)   FOR A WITNESS (2)
                                                R
Heat   Unclean
in the garden.   to your mind.

SEVENTH GEMATRIA
"Dreamers"

A DREAM (1)

It had ceased
in them.

A DREAM (2)

My great
heart.

A DREAM (3)

Without
God.

_____

NAKED

branches of
silver.

_____

THE BEARD (1)

Before you.

THE BEARD (2)

In the tree.

_____

TO ONE MADE SICK

in a dream.

THE RAVEN (1)

At evening.

THE RAVEN (2)

His voice
emptied out.

THE RAVEN (3)

Double
its color.

A FINGER

only
by its tail.

THE BREASTS

Inflamed
& scabby.

IN RIDDLES (1)

His word
has multiplied.

_____

GEMATRIA 309

A field
within her.

.

The stars,
a calf,
& an earring.

_____

TESTICLES

like fire.

_____

IN RIDDLES (2)

His word
is strange.

THE MOON (1)

We dreamed
our bread

Their genitals
stiffen.

.

The teeth
hard & cruel.

YESTERDAY (1)

The service.

THE YOUNG MEN

The birds.

THE MOON (2)

Who touches
the toucher.

YESTERDAY (2)

Her foot
between his knees.

AN EMPTY TOOTH

Dust
shining.

STARS

In his mouth.

SODOM (1)	SODOM (2)
A resting place.	Your blood.

SODOM (3)

According to his dream.

WE SHALL EAT

We ate.

AN EYE

Violets.
Jasmine.

HORSES

& a cloud.

A MOTHER (1)   A MOTHER (2)

Eve, or   A tree which bears
the Falcon.   no fruit.

WE DREAMED

& he changed.

EIGHTH GEMATRIA
"Things"

WOOD (1)

Heaped up.

WOOD (2)

He has chosen.

_____

SCARLET

Except for
the bottle.

_____

QUICK FLESH

High places.

_____

THE FIRST

Rings
shall hang.

.

Double
rings.

A DIVORCE

Hats
& gashes.

SETTINGS

The woman.
The eggs.
An old father.

SECRETLY

Ships.

.

You shall steal.

GEMATRIA 162

In the tree.
In the rock.

In the image.
In the money.

ROUNDABOUT KNOWLEDGE

A frying pan.

The bells
from the river.

.

A light
from the east.

GEMATRIA 1030

Three
for six.

WIDOWS

& hats.

LIKE A DEAD MAN

Your tool
will enlarge.

CHANGES (1)

A face.
A wheel.
A ladder.
A bone.

_____

dust, earth

.

onyx / empty

_____

GEMATRIA 618

A field
& its flowers.

.

The fat ones.

_____

CHANGES (2)

You will make it profane.

HOUSES

Within.

GEMATRIA 643

In the visions.
In the mirrors.

TWIN GEMATRIA

(1)
Eight
with trumpets.

(2)
Trumpets
& eight.

GEMATRIA 750

Two
thoughts.

Two
horns.

A year
from the city.

THE END (1)

The fair
days.

THE END (2)

The beautiful
waters.

THE END (3)

Her sweet
mouth.

GREENLY

Sarah
shot forth.

NINTH GEMATRIA
"God"

GOD

is not.

IN THE VALLEY (1)
High.

IN THE VALLEY (2)
Look!

GEMATRIA 20

The falcon.
The hooks.

.

His hands
will swoop down.

HIS SIN (1)

The beloved.

HIS SIN (2)

He loves
a fish.

YOUR FATHER

Your enemy.

GOD (1)

A flame.

GOD (2)

A terror.

A BOY CHILD

His father
will gore.

SACRIFICE (1)   SACRIFICE (2)

A goat.   The fish.

SACRIFICE (3)

Alas.

_____

THE FAT

& the poor.

_____

His glory
weeping?

.

His robes.

_____

THE BEAST (1)

An altar.

THE BEAST (2)

On a pole.

THE BEAST (3)

Devoured.

_____

THE HANGED MAN

will die.

_____

THE PROPHET (1)

shall lead.

THE PROPHET (2)

& the sand lizard.

THE PROPHET (3)

Someone
slain.

_____

MORE

Your feet
on the earth.

GEMATRIA 77

Your corn.
Your mercy.

Your mercy.
Your altar.

MY WRATH

& an emerald.

A PRIEST (1)

Against her children.

A PRIEST (2)

But the hands.

THE NURSING FATHER

Indeed.

THE WATER (1)

Waters.

THE WATER (2)

Seas.

YOUR KING

begot all.

GEMATRIA 106

Your servants.
Your god.

Your god.
His hand.

AN OFFERING (1)

I will eat
your heart.

AN OFFERING (2)

A raw
dog.

TENTH GEMATRIA
"Nations"

THE GOYIM (1)   THE GOYIM (2)

like the sand.   Their brothers.

THE GOYIM (3)

We are undone.

———————————————

GEMATRIA 112

To make bricks
of the people.

To make bricks
in your mouth.

———————————————

THE PEOPLE

The lice.

———————————————

CIRCUMCISED (1)

A blemish.

_____

THE PRIESTS

Because of
a plague.

_____

SINAI (1)

A ladder.

_____

GEMATRIA 132

To our god
from his servants.

To Baal
to our god.

_____

CIRCUMCISED (2)

Is it too hard?

SINAI (2)

Perhaps.

FOR A SIGN (1)

A fountain.

FOR A SIGN (2)

Wine &
pitch.

MINE EYES

Mine affliction.

ANGELS (1)

Messengers.

ANGELS (2)

Again.

GEMATRIA 142

In the basin.
In my eyes.

In my eyes.
In your bowels.

TO MY VOICE

Dumb
with sorrow.

_____

GEMATRIA 146

His face.
My voice.

My voice.
His eyes.

_____

THE OLD MAN (1)

A throne
to divide.

THE OLD MAN (2)

& night
like the day.

_____

OVER THE BIRDS

A white
tower.

_____

BECAUSE (1)

God is
a blemish.

BECAUSE (2)

Her nose
shall be circumcised.

BECAUSE (3)

A baker
did bake.

HE FLASHED LIGHT

with his finger.

GEMATRIA 206

A word
spoken.

A pestilence.

A thing.

A SHEKEL

A soul.

THEIR MONEY (1)

Shining.

THEIR MONEY (2)

A waste.

GEMATRIA 303

His neck.
Your arm.

His treasure.
Your feet.

A NUMBER (1)

Nothing
but God.

A NUMBER (2)

Our oppression.

ELEVENTH GEMATRIA
"Wilderness"

WHEN HE DIED:

My spirit was angry.

HIS SPIRIT (1)

He lighted
a pole.

HIS SPIRIT (2)

Like a mouth
on my hand.

NORTHWARD

& afterward.

A WOUND (1)

A pillar
& arrows.

A WOUND (2)

My thigh.

———————————

Like iron
& slime.

———————————

WORDS (1)   WORDS (2)

In the wilderness.   Shall we speak?

WORDS (3)

They will stone me.

———————————

GEMATRIA 251
            for Edmond Jabès

The desert
speaks.

———————————

A MULTITUDE (1)   A MULTITUDE (2)

Their anger   Thousands of
for food.   messengers.

84

GEMATRIA 259

In a coffin.
In the ark.

In the ark.
In the wilderness.

CHERUBIM

My horse
commanded them.

GEMATRIA 286

His city
& a city
& cities of
his city.

EVENING (1)   EVENING (2)

For the light.   Burnt out.

           EVENING (3)

             In passing.

————————————————

TO CLEANSE THEM:

Standing
in the basin.

————————————————

GEMATRIA 288

Buds

from the womb

had budded.

————————————————

A PREY (1)   A PREY (2)

Torn in pieces.   Plucked.

BE FRUITFUL

with a fist!

EVIL (1)   EVIL (2)

A city.   Eyes of
                    kings.

Sodden, cooked
lambs.

IMAGINATION (1)   IMAGINATION (2)

Surely.   Vain.

IMAGINATION (3)

Empty.

DOMINION

His parable.

FINS / TEETH

A bone
they scrape off.

FLESH (1)   FLESH (2)

& its flesh-hooks.   that lusted.

        FLESH (3)

        Enclosed.

TWELFTH GEMATRIA
"Imagination"

IMAGINATION (1)

IMAGINATION (2)

A wing'd
shoe.

Spices
ascending.

IMAGINATION (3)

A nest
that raised you up.

_____

IN THE MIDST (1)

IN THE MIDST (2)

In the morning.

In the grave.

_____

DARKNESS

& a lamb.

_____

TWIN GEMATRIA

Seventy
according to their number.

Blue
according to their tongues.

THOU, THEE

& he kissed him.

A PERVERSION

She was afraid
& he woke up.

GEMATRIA 404
"A Sodomite"

My angel.
Your anger.

Your anger.
His mouth.

———————————

ROUND ABOUT

According to its borders.

———————————

MYRIADS (1-3)

To remove
a foreskin:

grass
on your feet

& the purple
lamb.

———————————

SKIN HARPS

from my flesh.

EUPHRATES, EUPHRATES

Thirty
cows

grope
in the plains:

Euphrates
Euphrates.

GEMATRIA 692

A scar.
A quarter.

A fortified
scar.

WRITTEN

Wreathen.

PENETRATING STREAKS (1 & 2)

Three
lights

& three
horsemen.

GEMATRIA 806

(1)
Old
jars.

(2)
Doing it
roughly.

---

with lips

of linen

& crushed.

EIGHT

Eight.
Eight.

Double
eight.

IN BLUE (1)   IN BLUE (2)

Her breasts   Her breasts
were done.   for you.

          IN BLUE (3)

          For thee.
          For thee.

PHILISTINES

& their pins.

GEMATRIA 906
"Scarlet"

(1)
Scarlet
shoulder pieces.

(2)
Scarlet
& scarlet.

RED DREAMS

Flashing up.

GEMATRIA 1212
"His Desire"

(1)
She saw
streaks.

(2)
Bones
& a turtledove.

(3)
Holy.
Holy.
Holy.

MORE GEMATRIAS
1–100

1

His red
unclean
blood.
Earth
& water.
The adam, the man.
Fat
& bloody.   [50]

2

THE ANGEL (1)   THE ANGEL (2)

A star   His king.
shall uncover.   [96]

3

GEMATRIA 105

Man,
the blasphemer.

Man
the bald locust.

4

YOUR STUFF

My stuff
is unclean.   [120]

5

THE PLAGUE

Hands
that begot thee.   [128]

6

A WIZARD (1)   A WIZARD (2)

Between me   Let us sacrifice
& Leah.   your son.
                                                         [144]

7

EAST

Night
in your hearts.   [149]

8

Benjamin,
the old man,

brought us up,
a living substance

in your sight,
like sheep

he has upheld
your flock—

out of the thousands
—& has brought

a sprig of calamus
& wormwood

money
in your eye

& birds
& from his people

in the tree
an unjust gain

they rose up,
they shall rise up   [161, 162]

9

STREAKED (1)   STREAKED (2)

Great   Be white
twisted cords.   & pipe.

          STREAKED (3)

          His throne
          is washed.   [174]

10

THE PREY / THE REFUGE

I will go out
into the water.   [184]

11

A BONE

against you.   [202]

12

TO CURSE YOU / A CHARM
for H.B.

(1)
Bloom
the unclean.

(2)
I will blot him out
with stones.

(3)
Sodom
in Sodom.   [210]

13

THE LIGHT

will multiply.   [212]

14

MY WORDS
        for Charles Olson

To see for oneself.   [216]

15

THE JEW (1)	THE JEW (2)
A bastard.	With guile.

[287]

16

GEMATRIA 300

A ransom
& a purple
candlestick
for sale.

The curtain
will set.

Empty, vain.

Only
balm
for your sake,

only
formed,
torn by beasts &
uncircumcised.

Imagination.

Pomegranates of
atonement.

17

GEMATRIA 308

He will bathe
with honey

perfumes

& at night
will return
bald
as an agate

his grave
near at hand.

18

RETURN! (1)   RETURN! (2)

& he returned.   & he stayed put.

[318]

19

LAST NIGHT

Guilty.   [341]

20

MOSES (1)   MOSES (2)

The legs.   The hoofs.

          MOSES (3)

          A bearded
          vulture.   [345]

21

THE NAME (1)   THE NAME (2)

The book.   There.

                                          [345]

22

FIVE (1)   FIVE (2)

like snow.   And they asked.

                                          [353]

23

MESSIAH

A snake.   [358]

24

GEMATRIA 366

Naked
& scarlet.

.

Naked
& leprous.

.

Naked
& old.

.

His horns
drop down.

25

A NUMBER (1)   A NUMBER (2)

Wailing   Numbered
a number.   the end.

                                        [368/380]

26

AGAINST A MAN

Those who hate him. [381]

27

WHETHER (1)   WHETHER (2)

Concerning.   On the left.

[411]

28

GEMATRIA 432

And they heard
your house

your household

the daughters of
your houses

their bodies
shameful

inside
a perversion
of the soul.

29

THE JUDGMENT (1)   THE JUDGMENT (2)

In a flame.   In your house.

                                        [434]

30

JUDITH

The hawk
chews
her eyes.   [435]

31

GEMATRIA 438
"An Inscription"

To this
with its life.

And Tubal
with his soul.

And your household
with their weeping.

*The written
power is gone.*

32

GEMATRIA 444

cakes

/

& cakes

/

& a cake of

33

DEATH (1)   DEATH (2)

Let him die.   The moon
                      like a stranger.

                                    [446]

34

GEMATRIA 456
"Fear"

You will become unclean
You will become unclean

You will defile yourselves
in uncleanness

You will go
You will die

You will die
in uncleanness

And she went
And he died

And he died
And it ended

35

A BURNING

Remember
a foot.   [466]

36

GEMATRIA 461

Loops of
loops.

Have I eaten
with you?

In her banishment.
Ships.

Loops of
loops.

I have eaten
my terror.

37

GEMATRIA 469

Your fathers
& their saddles.

Our fathers
in ships.

38

GEMATRIA 482
"A Prophecy"

when they are dead,
enclosed
among you,
white
in knowledge
& in booths,
you will wash
your daughters—
according to the writings
& the later rain

39

A CARCASS
Your first-born
has blessd you.   [484]

40

A BEAUTIFUL KNIFE

(1)
The curtain
& your eye.

(2)
Imagination
hidden.

(3)
We die
& are beautiful.   [496]

41

GEMATRIA 499

The frogs.

.

The hosts.

I call to witness.

42

GEMATRIA 506

Her head
giving suck.

Gall,
her food.

"I have served you
an ox.

Will you eat it?"

43

GEMATRIA 507

you will eat
her flesh,
her belly

& the poison
you will spew out
will consume us

& our lands:
you will eat it
& go forth

44

GEMATRIA 508

Silence.
A night hawk.

Black
wagons.

Deaf
flesh.

45

GEMATRIA 519
"Around Midnight"

so he drove out
& was silent

& she took it
& when it rose

sang
the song

at their door
around midnight

46

SUDDENLY

Their words are
a cry.   [521]

47

THE LANGUAGE OF THE BEES

He was silent.   [523]

48

LIKE HIS FLESH

Jordan
burning.   [528]

49

PIECES (1)   PIECES (2)

Removing   The vineyard
the pieces.   cried.
                                                [528]

50

FLESH (1)   FLESH (2)

Show me   A pillar.
an image.

    FLESH (3)

    Sold
    in the gutters.   [532]

51

KINGDOMS (1)   KINGDOMS (2)

He was angry.   She was despised.

    KINGDOMS (3)

    His kingdom.   [532]

52

TWINED

with its feathers.   [547]

53

GEMATRIA 548

A scab
from his flesh.

A sickle.

Trembling
at evening.

54

GEMATRIA 556

The first
worms
carry us up.

The remaining one
flies
your commandments.

55

YOUR LOINS

The thighs
he stripped naked.   [560]

56

GEMATRIA 560

Snow.

.

The evil
shepherd.

.

And at evening
their thighs.

57

SAD GEMATRIA

I am old

.

.

.

& I fell down.   [567]

58

GEMATRIA 570

Ten
fountains.

.

A hairy
bed.

.

Straight,
void,
fruitful,
smashed.

.

Hair
like an eagle.

59

FOUNTAINS

& wonders.   [576]

60

GEMATRIA 580

Serpents.

Asps.

Demons.

A fiery serpent.

61

GEMATRIA 582

flowers
torn in pieces

adornments of
the earth

62

GEMATRIA 586
"The Goat"

They blow
a horn

& burn
its dung.

63

BURNING

A light from
the river.   [590]

64

A SWARM (1)   A SWARM (2)

They shall spread.   More.

[596]

65

GEMATRIA 600

(1)
Eagles.

(2)
Eyes
kill
the light.

(3)
A fire
in his land.

(4)
See
the darkness.

(5)
Beautiful
Sodom.

(6)
Always
his eyes.

(7)
Angels of
bone
in your seed.

66

TWO GEMATRIAS FOR
THEODORE ENSLIN

Forms (1)

Imagination
a fire.

Forms (2)

The uncircumcised
rock.   [601]

67

GEMATRIA 610

(1)
Her mistress
greenish.
My bones
spread wide.

(2)
A tenth.
A tithe.
A sixth.
Ten thousands.

68

THE BRIGHT SPOT (1)

When he came down.

THE BRIGHT SPOT (2)

The fire
in his skin.

THE BRIGHT SPOT (3)

A woman like
honey.   [612]

69

A COVENANT (1)   A COVENANT (2)

A foreskin   A fake
restored.   foreskin.

                                        [612]

70

GEMATRIA 619

The spirits.
The end.

.

Plump
& fat.

71

THE LAST

like the first one.   [621]

72

TAMAR (1)   TAMAR (2)

A naked   Like the rain.
boy.   [640]

73

GEMATRIA 646

The lights
of his ribs.

74

GEMATRIA 655

The boards.
The lamps.

The turtledoves.
The demons.

And a deep sleep.

75

GEMATRIA 676

Nakedness.

Blindness.

They lay down
& he lay down.

I will hide.

76

GEMATRIA 678

As he fed
& was famished

you will kindle
& burn.

77

STRANGERS

she sent out
like spies.   [686]

78

GEMATRIA 690

Palm trees.

Candlesticks.

Curtains.

Hoof
of a lamb.

79

GEMATRIA 693
"The Hebrew Women"

His name
at noon.

.

Her name
far off.

.

Rejoice
in the lamb.

80

GEMATRIA 700

An ark cover.
A foreskin.

A foreskin.
A veil.

You have turned aside.

81

THE SABBATH

A tooth
for a tooth.   [702]

82

GEMATRIA 723

You will slaughter
& I will bring back.

You will slaughter
& you will sow.

You will slaughter
& you will slaughter.

83

GEMATRIA 730

You will lend upon interest.
You are covered with fat.

84

DIVINATION (1)   DIVINATION (2)

Ears of corn   Your bed
in the firmament.   like a bed.

[764]

85

GEMATRIA 780

Heaven.
He made you.

Oil.
From my book.

In the ashes.
Heaven.

Eleven.

Alone.

86

GEMATRIA 796

The maidservant
will lie with her.

.

Trumpets.

.

Out of his sleep.

.

The maidservant.

Send me away.

87

UNDER YOUR MAID

Be dismayed.
Be dismayed.   [808]

88

THANKSGIVING

Your lips.   [810]

89

GEMATRIA 828

Families
& jars.

And imprints
of families.

90

PHILISTINES

Shekels
for wives.   [860]

91

GEMATRIA 870

I had followed
a coat.

92

NETWORK (1)   NETWORK (2)

When you go.   Your soul
                      in fury.

          NETWORK (3)

          I started
          to write.

                                        [900]

93

GEMATRIA 904

(1)
According to their generations.

(2)
After their pattern.

(3)
By way of their families.

94

THE ACCOUNTING (1)   THE ACCOUNTING (2)

Have you stolen   Have you stolen
their sisters?   their sacks?

                                          [910]

95

IN PRAISE OF THE DEAD

That they will crawl.   [940]

96

TENS
  for David Meltzer

I prepared
the meathooks.

.

You guided
the timbrel.

.

It covered
the land.   [970]

138

97

GEMATRIA 980
"Burning"

You will burn
your wages.

.

A kid
will be burned.

.

Dead
in the entry.

98

GEMATRIA 988

I know
his dreams.

.

Stone
wombs.

Many
bruised testicles.

.

Almond blossoms.
Frogs.

.

And the open
door.

99

GEMATRIA 1082

a trumpet blast

/

first
the thunders

/

the thunders, the voices
& the thunders

100

CHAINS (1)   CHAINS (2)

Your six   False
gates.   eagles.   [1200]

BEYOND GEMATRIA

GEMATRIA ONE

Laughter. Of their blood into his nostrils. Numbed. And the window numbed as well. We ate the children. We will eat their gods. We ate & we will eat. His desire will be ransomed. May my angel eat? He may. He will. He will heave a bone against you. A sodomite & angel. The confusion arising from two kinds—of bones? of angels? When the water rises into waters. As when the water rises into seas.

GEMATRIA TWO

Perhaps they do,
millennial & white—
a kingdom talks to me   your bread
is taken for a treasure
—even more the lice—
stars shine in his mouth
beneath his gums
a yellow angel rises, swelling
like a bat
a great star, fair as days
& beautiful as waters,
as her sweet mouth haunts
the man who sees
& knows a window,
if an angel by himself
becomes a cup,
also a little owl,
my heart condenses to an emerald,
water that our hearts are,
eyes, a basket from the sea,
the face his mouth took for a king's
& saved although the face
kept murmuring, the sea
drove globulets onto the land,

his bone against her, wailing,
a star is in your mouth,
your yellow god is sucking
like a dog

GEMATRIA THREE

when he sent a curse
against you
with his finger, you saw
a cloud in wood,
streaked dainties
in the rain   the cloud
over his head was
empty, empty
was the vine,
your shoes were empty
& walking toward a flashing light
your eyes watched
the little numbers
wailing,
horses & a cloud,
a place *within* we asked
if we could find
& found a man who sat
astride a couch,
a man who flashes lights
& shakes a finger
like a blossom
numbering our days,
congealed
before it ends

GEMATRIA FOUR

your mistress
conceived   I did it

(she said) for his seed
& for the fire

a blessing
for twenty

you have blesst
the fat

& the fat ones
their droppings are clean

like a field
& its flowers

plump
& fat

"these you will number
& those I will kill"

GEMATRIA FIVE

The darkness
gushes against a second
darkness

blesst & scalded,
redder than the lamb the demons
bring, evil shepherds

who surround you,
turtledoves above & lamps
like stars, like lights

all over
the night sky,
glowing

as an oven fills with darkness,
the jews inside their cities
lost in sleep

GEMATRIA SIX

when he came down
she saw him
she saw streaks & bones

she saw a turtledove
his neck
was in the fire

zohar in the morning
bright spots
in the grave

false
cagles,
chains

my holiness remembered

GEMATRIA SEVEN

after the man removed his hat, his words
were suddenly a cry
his songs a horned snake

gods rushed against his doors
with slime, a face
became a wheel

bricks framed a ladder
there were hollow stones
& hooks & jewels

his daughters pitched their clothes
into the gutters
the widows sprang for hats

at midnight   he was silent
but retained a place & watched
the pieces fall behind him

the way a star falls in his dreams

DOMESTIC GEMATRIA
"Home Movies"

Inward,
in her house,
a beast
sinned,
souls fell lusting.
You shall bring
my sister.
(Yes.)
Your wives
like wives
—like birds inside
his house—
your daughter whom they stripped
& let her be.

A GEMATRIA FOR HORSEMEN

Three horsemen
will be cut off.

.

Three
& three.

To seek it out.
To see it.

To rejoice.

.

Three
fiery
horsemen.

.

Three
for six.

.

The horsemen.
Three.

.

I have cut a covenant
for six

& I will come down
falsely.

KHURBN GEMATRIA [266]

1

The oppression
will smite

the camp
with thirst

& dust:
the plague

is in your barns
the camp

delivered
to their gods

2

a wheel
dyed red

an apparition

set apart

out of the furnace

3

from his youth
she bound him

afterwards
they turned aside
& went

his streams
their vineyards

an apparition
that was at the end

sold
in the gutters

"show me"

"I will turn aside"

PAPER AIRS

A GAME OF CARDS

Pharaoh.
Faro.
Landing lights.

DISGUST

The sky clears up,
uncramps him.

TRANSITIONS

Ballistics.

THE ONE-EYED MAN

takes out the stains:
malpractice!

TIRE TREADS

Space.
Room.
Duration.
Time.

THE DREAMER

From dictation,
pawns his heart.

A FLOWER-HOLDER

Just like me.

THE EXPEDITION

starts an anchor
like a trowel,
soon transplaced.

PAPER AIRS

They beat the ground
for animals.
They round up thieves.

THE QUESTION

Torture as
constraint. He makes himself
at home.

AN EARLY PEAR

In my opinion.

IN THE COOL OF THE EVENING

There is nothing for you here
the chauffeur grumbles. *Who
has pinched my matches?*

GREMLINS

Licorice as sex.

COLD RIVETS

COLD RIVETS

Third year syllabus.

OLD AGE

Stand by the wall.
Sit at the window.
At the scene of the crime.

ECLIPSE

A foot stands in the doorway.

THE DAY OF REST

A bonfire.
Howls or shrieks of joy.

A MORAL COWARD

He eats a cold meal in the evening.

BLOOD CLOT

A pebble.
Broken flint.
The art of driving.

TORPOR

At the point of death.

A LITTLE MAN

Sweat rolling off
his forehead, raining
on the priest.

THIEVES

With solemn manners.
Hooks set in squares.

THE WHIP

This wall obstructs the view.

LINES COMPOSED ACCORDING
TO THE LAWS OF CHANCE

A horn blows in my ears.
The whole town's talking.
When the fruit turns red.

THE DEMIGOD (1)

lies waiting,
drunk & gay,
run down by horses.

THE DEMIGOD (2)

Old gelding
founders.

PROGRESS
for Barrett Watten
Apple fritters.

A HINT

Provokes to anger.
Burning.
Glowing.
Dynamite.
The golden mean.

PLURALITIES

They strip the flesh off.
Tear the clothes to shreds.

NATURAL HISTORY (1)

of ropes & cables.

NATURAL HISTORY (2)

Going downstream
like a cushion.

NATURAL HISTORY (3)

distracts me.

NATURAL HISTORY (4)

Construction of a sentence.
On a map.

NOTHING

A country full of woods.
An empty belly.

POST/FACE

Gematria—a form of traditional Jewish numerology—
plays off the fact that every letter of the Hebrew alphabet
is also a number, & that words or phrases the sums of
whose letters are equal are at some level meaningfully
connected. In the foregoing poems I have been working
from the over three hundred pages of word lists that
make up Gutman G. Locks's *The Spice of Torah—Gema-
tria* (Judaica Press, New York, 1985), which offer easy
access to the numerical value of every word in the first
five books of the Hebrew Bible. Unlike the traditionalists
of gematria, I have seen these coincidences/synchronicities
not as hermeneutic substantiations for religious and ethi-
cal doctrines, but as an entry into the kinds of correspon-
dences/constellations that have been central to modernist
& "post" modernist poetry experiments over the last cen-
tury & a half. I have proceeded in these works in several
different ways: by using one word or word-phrase as title
and others (numerically equivalent) as poem; by using the
gematria number as a title & constructing poems of sin-
gle lines and/or stanzas of two or several lines that fall
under or add up to that number; & in the section titled
"Beyond Gematria," by using a freer selection of words
brought to my attention by gematria, but combining &
adding to them with considerably more freedom of
choice. (While the last two series presented here—"Paper
Airs" & "Cold Rivets"—are not gematrias as such, they

seem to me to be related both in language & intention.)
Several gematria poems are dedicated to contemporary &
predecessor poets, because they involve words that have
some connection to poems written or poetics practiced by
those poets. To the degree that all the works in this gath-
ering are substantially aleatory, they are full of surprises
that have added greatly to my own excitement in the
process of composition. At any rate I feel that the process
used, in this case at least, is not irrelevant to a reading of
the resulting poems.

JEROME ROTHENBERG

Encinitas, California

Jerome Rothenberg

Jerome Rothenberg is the author of over fifty books of poetry, including *Poems for the Game of Silence, Poland/1931, New Selected Poems, Khurbn,* and *The Lorca Variations* (all from New Directions). Actively engaged in poetry and performance since the late 1950s, he has also edited six ground-breaking anthologies of experimental and traditional poetry, including *Technicians of the Sacred, Shaking the Pumpkin,* and *A Big Jewish Book* (a.k.a. *Exiled in the Word*). He recently co-edited and translated, with Pierre Joris, a volume of "poems performance pieces proses plays poetics" by Kurt Schwitters, and he is working with Joris on a global anthology of twentieth-century experimental poetry to be published by the University of California Press.

Kenneth Rexroth wrote of him: "Jerome Rothenberg is one of the truly contemporary American poets who has returned U.S. poetry to the mainstream of international modern literature. . . . No one writing poetry today has dug deeper into the roots of poetry."

SUN & MOON CLASSICS

The Sun & Moon Classics is a publicly supported, nonprofit program to publish new editions, translations, or republications of outstanding world literature of the late nineteenth and twentieth centuries. Through its publication of living authors as well as great masters of the century, the series attempts to redefine what usually is meant by the idea of a "classic" by dehistoricizing the concept and embracing a new, ever changing literary canon.

Organized by the Contemporary Arts Educational Project, Inc., a nonprofit corporation, and published by its program Sun & Moon Press, the series is made possible, in part, by grants and individual contributions.

This book was made possible, in part, through matching grants from the National Endowment for the Arts and from the California Arts Council, through an organizational grant from the Andrew W. Mellon Foundation, through a grant for advertising and promotion from the Lila Wallace/Reader's Digest Fund, and through contributions from the following individuals:

Charles Altieri (Seattle, Washington)
John Arden (Galway, Ireland)
Jesse Huntley Ausubel (New York, New York)
Dennis Barone (West Hartford, Connecticut)
Jonathan Baumbach (Brooklyn, New York)
Guy Bennett (Los Angeles, California)
Bill Berkson (Bolinas, California)
Steve Benson (Berkeley, California)
Charles Bernstein and Susan Bee (New York, New York)
Sherry Bernstein (New York, New York)
Dorothy Bilik (Silver Spring, Maryland)
Bill Corbett (Boston, Massachusetts)
Fielding Dawson (New York, New York)
Robert Crosson (Los Angeles, California)
Tina Darragh and P. Inman (Greenbelt, Maryland)
David Detrich (Los Angeles, California)
Christopher Dewdney (Toronto, Canada)
Philip Dunne (Malibu, California)
George Economou (Norman, Oklahoma)
Elaine Equi and Jerome Sala (New York, New York)
Lawrence Ferlinghetti (San Francisco, California)
Richard Foreman (New York, New York)
Howard N. Fox (Los Angeles, California)
Jerry Fox (Aventura, Florida)

In Memoriam: Rose Fox
Melvyn Freilicher (San Diego, California)
Miro Gavran (Zagreb, Croatia)
Peter Glassgold (Brooklyn, New York)
Barbara Guest (New York, New York)
Perla and Amiram V. Karney (Bel Air, California)
Fred Haines (Los Angeles, California)
Fanny Howe (La Jolla, California)
Harold Jaffe (San Diego, California)
Ira S. Jaffe (Albuquerque, New Mexico)
Alex Katz (New York, New York)
Tom LaFarge (New York, New York)
Mary Jane Lafferty (Los Angeles, California)
Michael Lally (Santa Monica, California)
Norman Lavers (Jonesboro, Arkansas)
Jerome Lawrence (Malibu, California)
Stacey Levine (Seattle, Washington)
Herbert Lust (Greenwich, Connecticut)
Norman MacAffee (New York, New York)
Rosemary Macchiavelli (Washington, DC)
Beatrice Manley (Los Angeles, California)
Martin Nakell (Los Angeles, California)
Toby Olson (Philadelphia, Pennsylvania)
Maggie O'Sullivan (Hebden Bridge, England)
Rochelle Owens (Norman, Oklahoma)
Marjorie and Joseph Perloff (Pacific Palisades, California)
Dennis Phillips (Los Angeles, California)
David Reed (New York, New York)
Ishmael Reed (Oakland, California)
Janet Rodney (Santa Fe, New Mexico)
Joe Ross (Washington, DC)
Dr. Marvin and Ruth Sackner (Miami Beach, Florida)
Floyd Salas (Berkeley, California)
Tom Savage (New York, New York)
Leslie Scalapino (Oakland, California)
James Sherry (New York, New York)
Aaron Shurin (San Francisco, California)
Charles Simic (Strafford, New Hampshire)
Gilbert Sorrentino (Stanford, California)
Catharine R. Stimpson (Staten Island, New York)
John Taggart (Newburg, Pennsylvania)
Nathaniel Tarn (Tesuque, New Mexico)

Fiona Templeton (New York, New York)
Mitch Tuchman (Los Angeles, California)
Wendy Walker (New York, New York)
Anne Walter (Carnac, France)
Arnold Wesker (Hay on Wye, England)

If you would like to be a contributor to this series, please send your tax-deductible contribution to The Contemporary Arts Educational Project, Inc., a non-profit corporation, 6026 Wilshire Boulevard, Los Angeles, California 90036.

*First American publication
**Revised edition